P9-ARV-166

Snack Attack:
Unhealthy Treats

Slim Goodbody's
LIGHTEN UP
SERIES

Crabtree Publishing Company
www.crabtreebooks.com

Series Development and Packaging: John Burstein, Slim Goodbody Corp.
Senior Script Development: Phoebe Backler
Managing Editor: Valerie J. Weber
Designer and Illustrator: Ben McGinnis
Graphic Design Agency: Adventure Advertising
Instructional Designer: Alan Backler, Ph. D.
Content Consultant: Betty Hubbard, Ed. D., Certified Health Education Specialist
Project Editor: Reagan Miller

Library and Archives Canada Cataloguing in Publication

Burstein, John.
    Snack attack : unhealthy treats / Slim Goodbody.

(Slim Goodbody's lighten up!)
ISBN 978-0-7787-3918-0 (bound).--ISBN 978-0-7787-3936-4 (pbk.)

    1. Nutrition--Juvenile literature. 2. Snack foods--Juvenile literature.
I. Title. II. Series: Goodbody, Slim. Slim Goodbody's lighten up!
RA784.G675 2008   j613.2
C2008-900727-1

Library of Congress Cataloging-in-Publication Data

Burstein, John.
    Snack attack : unhealthy treats / John Burstein.
      p. cm. -- (Slim goodbody's lighten up!)
    Includes index.
    ISBN-13: 978-0-7787-3918-0 (rlb)
    ISBN-10: 0-7787-3918-X (rlb)
    ISBN-13: 978-0-7787-3936-4 (pb)
    ISBN-10: 0-7787-3936-8 (pb)
    1. Nutrition--Juvenile literature. 2. Snack foods--Juvenile literature. I.
Title. II. Series.

    RA784.B793 2008
    613.2--dc22
                        2008003597

Crabtree Publishing Company

www.crabtreebooks.com   1-800-387-7650

Copyright © **2008 CRABTREE PUBLISHING COMPANY.** All rights reserved. No part of this publication may be reproduced, stored in a retrieval system or be transmitted in any form or by any means, electronic, mechanical, photocopying, recording, or otherwise, without the prior written permission of Crabtree Publishing Company. In Canada: We acknowledge the financial support of the Government of Canada through the Book Publishing Industry Development Program (BPIDP) for our publishing activities.

Published in Canada
Crabtree Publishing
616 Welland Ave.
St. Catharines, Ontario
L2M 5V6

Published in the United States
Crabtree Publishing
PMB16A
350 Fifth Ave., Suite 3308
New York, NY 10118

Published in the United Kingdom
Crabtree Publishing
White Cross Mills
High Town, Lancaster
LA1 4XS

Published in Australia
Crabtree Publishing
386 Mt. Alexander Rd.
Ascot Vale (Melbourne)
VIC 3032

"Slim Goodbody" and "Lighten Up with Slim Goodbody" are registered trademarks of the Slim Goodbody Corp.

Printed in the U.S.A.

TABLE OF CONTENTS

HELLO THERE. I'M SLIM GOODBODY,

and my greatest goal in life is to help young people across the planet become healthy and active. After all, one in three kids in the United States is overweight. Without changing their eating and exercise habits, many of these young people will become overweight adults. They risk many possible health problems like **high blood pressure** or **diabetes**.

Today, I would like to introduce you to my friend Alexis. Alexis loves to explore the outdoors and rock climb with her brother, Sam. In school, she and her friends are in a **nutrition** club. They have worked on all sorts of projects to help educate the other students about eating healthy food. They still have one challenge left, however. The vending machines at school sell junk food. Follow Alexis and her friends as they try to find a way to offer healthy snacks to their friends and teachers.

Smart Snacking

Hi, my name is Alexis. I love to explore the wilderness and rock climb. My older brother, Sam taught me how to have fun and stay safe in the woods. Sam is in college. He's majoring in nutrition so he's also taught me a lot about the importance of eating healthy food. This summer, before Sam went back to college, we gathered up our gear and went to our favorite rock-climbing spot.

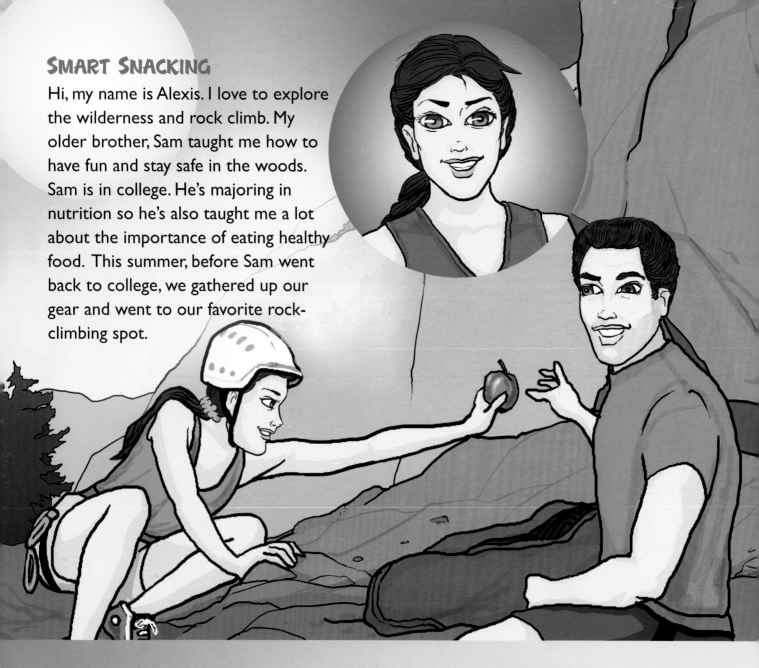

Get Ready to Climb!

At the bottom of the cliff, Sam pulled open his backpack. "Let's eat something before we start climbing. I don't want to get halfway up and realize I don't have any energy left!"

"Yeah, that would be a drag," I said as he handed me an apple.

"You know, before I got to college, I never realized what a difference it makes to eat healthy snacks. I eat something small every three or four hours, and then I don't overeat at meals. I used to be so hungry by lunch and dinner that I would eat mountains of food," said Sam. "Healthy snacks give me a lot more energy too."

"I always thought that snacking was bad," I said as I finished my apple and started putting on my climbing harness and climbing shoes. "Mom always says that snacks spoil your appetite for meals."

THE RIGHT SNACKS

"Well, you shouldn't eat snacks right before meals, and you have to be careful about what you eat," advised Sam. "Steer clear of those **pre-packaged snacks** that have a ton of **calories** and not many **nutrients**. I learned in one of my classes that kids get about 25 percent of their calories from snacks. That's why it's so important to teach kids about eating healthy snack foods."

"Yeah. All the kids at my school eat those pre-packaged chocolate-covered granola bars," I told him.

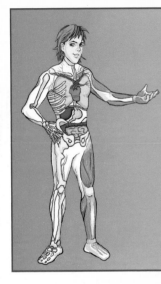

Slim Goodbody Says: Many scientists believe that young people in the United States are becoming overweight because they eat so many pre-packaged snacks and drink so much soda and sugary juices. Many of those snacks and drinks are high in calories because they have additional sweeteners, such as sugar and high-fructose corn syrup. Other added sweeteners include fruit-juice concentrates, maltose, dextrose, sucrose, honey, and maple syrup. Unfortunately, these pre-packaged snacks and sugary beverages are also low in important vitamins and minerals. If you have many of these snacks and beverages, you will gain weight without getting the nutrients you need to stay healthy and grow strong.

"That's too bad," said Sam. "But hey, we're here to climb, not talk, right? Are you ready?" He hooked up ropes at the top of the cliff so we would be safe. When he was finished, I started climbing.

Far above the ground, I looked out to the beautiful view of mountains behind me. "Wow! It's incredible up here!" I shouted to Sam. When I got back down, I exclaimed, "I forgot how hard that climb is! I'm glad I had that apple first!"

GET GOING WITH *GO* SNACKS

As I untied the rope from my harness, I said, "I was thinking about what you said earlier about eating healthy snacks. Last year, my friends and I started a nutrition club at school. We worked on getting healthier food in the cafeteria. The problem is that we still have vending machines that are full of junk food."

"That's really cool that you're trying to get the school to offer healthier food," said Sam.

"Do you have any ideas for how our club can teach other students about eating better snacks?" I asked.

GOOD *GO* FOODS

"Well, one of my teachers at college talks a lot about *Go, Slow,* and *Whoa* foods," Sam said.

"What are they?" I asked.

"*Go* foods are low in fat and sugar. They have fewer calories too, and they're full of healthy vitamins, minerals, and other nutrients. Some people think that healthy food tastes bad, but they're really wrong. All sorts of *Go* foods taste great and give you lots of energy," said Sam.

"So what would you consider *Go* foods?" I asked.

"Most fruits and vegetables are *Go* foods. Whole-grain cereals are too as long as they aren't sugary. Whole-grain pastas and low-fat yogurt and cheeses are *Go* foods too," said Sam.

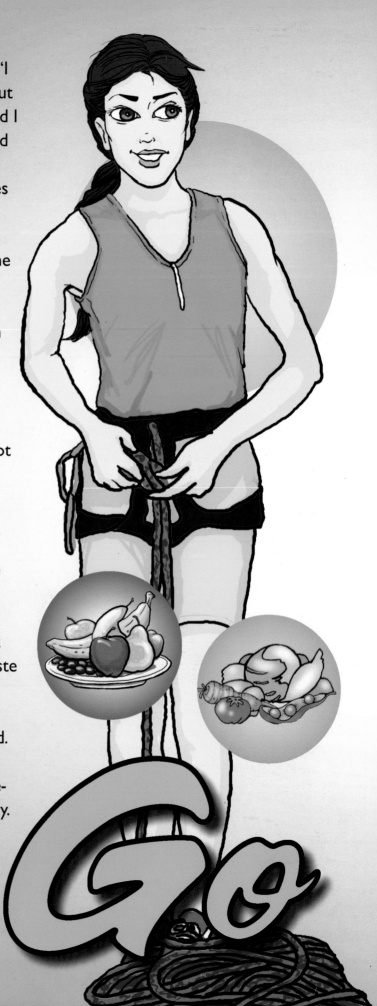

Slim Goodbody Says: Fruits and vegetables are good for you fresh, frozen, or canned. Make sure to choose canned fruit that is packaged in fruit juice, not sugary syrup.

"So how can you tell if a cereal is a *Go* food?" I asked.

"Packaged foods have Nutrition Facts labels on the back. They have all the information you need to tell if food is healthy or not," explained Sam.

Slim Goodbody Says: Nutrition Facts labels tell you how many calories and nutrients are in one serving of food. For example, if you are wondering how much **calcium** is in a serving of this yogurt, you can look at the bottom of the label. You will see that the yogurt contains 45 percent of the calcium that you need in one day. This number is called the **Percent Daily Value**. The Percent Daily Value is based on a 2,000-calorie diet. If you eat two servings of this yogurt, you will have eaten almost all the calcium that your body needs for the whole day.

Do you think that this yogurt is a Go food?
Use this chart to help you decide if it is.

Go Foods Contain
• 0 to 100 calories
• less than 5 percent of bad nutrients like **sodium**, and **cholesterol**
• 20 percent or more good nutrients like vitamins, minerals, and **fiber**

This yogurt has no fat, a moderate number of calories, and, of course, 45 percent of the calcium you need in a day. Do you think it is a *Go* food? You're right! It is!

Nutrition Facts

Serving Size 1 container (226g)

Amount Per Serving	
Calories 100	Calories from Fat 0

	% Daily Value*
Total Fat 0g	0%
Saturated Fat 0g	0%
Cholesterol less than 5mg	1%
Sodium 160mg	7%
Total Carbohydrate 15g	5%
Dietary Fiber 0g	0%
Sugars 10g	
Protein 13g	

Vitamin A 0%	•	Vitamin C 4%
Calcium 45%	•	Iron 0%

*Percent Daily Values are based on a 2,000 calorie diet. Your daily values may be higher or lower depending on your calorie needs.

7

SLOW DOWN ON THE *SLOW* SNACKS

"So what are *Slow* foods?" I asked.

"*Slow* foods are higher in fat and added sugar than *Go* foods. They also have more calories so it's a good idea to eat them less often than *Go* foods," explained Sam.

"What do you consider *Slow* food?" I asked.

"Well, oven-baked French fries, low-fat ice cream, waffles, and pancakes are all *Slow* foods," Sam told me.

 **Slim Goodbody Says:** Other examples of *Slow* foods are dried fruit, low-fat peanut butter, and frozen fruit-juice bars.

LOOK AT THE LABEL

"And can you tell from the Nutrition Facts label that *Slow* foods aren't as healthy as *Go* foods?" I asked him.

"You bet," said Sam. "You can also look at the ingredients list. The food's ingredients that weigh the most are at the beginning of the list. So if added sweeteners and oils are the first ingredients on the list, you know the snack is unhealthy," he explained.

"People who eat too many foods that are high in fat, calories, and sweeteners can become overweight. As a result, they have a higher chance of having health problems like diabetes and high blood pressure," Sam continued

"Now, step aside, it's my turn to climb!" Sam said with a grin. I watched Sam skillfully climb to the top of the cliff. He then lowered himself down in one smooth motion.

Slim Goodbody Says: Take a look at this Nutrition Facts label, and answer this quiz. Use the *Slow* foods chart below to help you.

1. What's the **serving size** for this snack?
2. How many calories does it have per serving?
3. What is the Percent Daily Value of saturated fat?
4. Does it contain a significant amount of vitamins, minerals, and fiber?
5. Is this a *Slow* food?

Slow Foods Contain

- 100 to 400 calories
- between 5 percent and 20 percent of unhealthy nutrients like fat, sodium, and cholesterol
- between 5 percent and 20 percent of healthy nutrients like vitamins, minerals, and fiber

Nutrition Facts

Serving Size 1 cup (228g)
Servings Per Container 2

Amount Per Serving	
Calories 250	Calories from Fat 110

	% Daily Value*
Total Fat 12g	18%
Saturated Fat 3g	15%
Trans Fat 3g	
Cholesterol 30mg	10%
Sodium 390mg	16%
Total Carbohydrate 31g	10%
Dietary Fiber 2g	8%
Sugars 5g	
Protein 5g	

Vitamin A	7%
Vitamin C	6%
Calcium	19%
Iron	6%

*Percent Daily Values are based on a 2,000 calorie diet. Your daily values may be higher or lower depending on your calorie needs.

	Calories	2,000	2,500
Total Fat	Less than	65g	80g
Sat Fat	Less than	20g	25g
Cholesterol	Less than	300mg	300mg
Sodium	Less than	2,400mg	2,400mg
Total Carbohydrate		300g	375g
Dietary Fiber		25g	30g

Answers:1. One cup (228 grams) 2. 250 3. 15 percent 4.Yes 5.Yes

WHOA THERE WITH THOSE WHOA SNACKS!

A few weeks later, I was back in school. While waiting for our first class one morning, my friends and I talked about our nutrition club.

"I've got a new idea for our club!" I said, excitedly. "I think that we should try to get rid of junk food in the vending machines!"

"I totally agree," said my friend Stacey. "There isn't a single healthy snack in those machines. What if you're hungry before lunch and you've forgotten to bring something from home? Your only choices are candy bars and potato chips."

WHAT ARE WHOA FOODS?

"Yeah and those are *Whoa* foods," I added.

"What?" my friends asked, looking confused.

I smiled, "My brother studies nutrition in college. He calls foods that are high in fat, sugar, and calories like potato chips, doughnuts, and candy bars, '*Whoa* foods.' They fill you up without giving you any of the nutrients that help keep you healthy and strong."

 Slim Goodbody Says: Whole milk, cheeses, cookies, cake, ice cream, and chicken nuggets are other examples of *Whoa* foods. You should only eat *Whoa* foods every once in a while.

"Yeah, but if those foods are in the vending machine, kids will be tempted to buy them," said Cameron, another friend.

"I think it's a great idea, Alexis. Let's try to convince the school to put healthy snacks in the vending machines!" said Stacey.

Ice Cream Pop

Nutrition Facts
Serving Size 1 pop • 45g

Amount Per Serving

Calories 420   Calories from Fat 225

	% Daily Value*
Total Fat 25g	38%
Saturated Fat 14g	70%
Cholesterol 55mg	18%
Sodium 145mg	6%
Total Carbohydrate 44g	15%
Dietary Fiber 0g	0%
Soluble Fiber 0g	
Insoluble Fiber 0g	
Sugars 34g	
Protein 5g	10%

Vitamin A 15% •	Vitamin C 0%
Calcium 10%	Iron 6%

Mini Pretzel Twists

Nutrition Facts
Serving Size 45g (about 33 pieces)

Amount Per Serving

Calories 100   Calories from Fat 15

	% Daily Value*
Total Fat 1.5g	2%
Saturated Fat 0g	0%
Cholesterol 60mg	20%
Sodium 300mg	12%
Total Carbohydrate 63g	21%
Dietary Fiber 0g	0%
Soluble Fiber 0g	
Insoluble Fiber 0g	
Sugars 29g	
Protein 4g	8%

Vitamin A 0% •	Vitamin C 0%
Calcium 4%	Iron 0%

Baked Potato Chips

Nutrition Facts
Serving Size 45g (about 15 chips)

Amount Per Serving

Calories 180   Calories from Fat 45

	% Daily Value*
Total Fat 6g	9%
Saturated Fat 0g	0%
Cholesterol 60mg	20%
Sodium 300mg	12%
Total Carbohydrate 63g	21%
Dietary Fiber 0g	0%
Soluble Fiber 0g	
Insoluble Fiber 0g	
Sugars 29g	
Protein 4g	8%

Vitamin A 0% •	Vitamin C 0%
Calcium 4%	Iron 0%

Slim Goodbody Says: Compare these snacks and decide if they are *Go, Slow,* or *Whoa* foods. Notice that the serving size for each of the snacks is similar. A similar size means that you can compare them more easily.

Use this chart for help:

Go Foods	*Slow* Foods	*Whoa* Foods
0-100 calories	100-400 calories	400 calories or more
5 percent or fewer of bad nutrients, such as fat, sodium, and cholesterol	Between 5 and 20 percent of bad nutrients, such as fat, sodium, and cholesterol	More than 20 percent of bad nutrients, such as fat, sodium, and cholesterol
20 percent or more good nutrients, such as vitamins, minerals, and fiber	Between 5 and 20 percent of good nutrients, such as vitamins, minerals and fiber	less than 5 percent of good nutrients, such as vitamins, minerals, and fiber

Remember, not all of the nutrients in a food will fit perfectly into these ranges for *Go, Slow,* and *Whoa* foods. The most important thing is that you look to see that a food is low in fat, calories, and sodium and make sure it has a healthy amount of fiber and some vitamins and minerals.

Answers: The ice cream pop is a *Whoa* food, the baked potato chips are a *Slow* food, and the mini pretzel twists are a *Go* food.

Go, Slow, and Whoa Beverages

As we walked to class, we passed the vending machines in the hall.

"Shouldn't we try to do something about the soda machines too?" asked Stacey.

I agreed, "Yeah. Soda is a *Whoa* food for sure."

Soda Versus Juice

Our first class of the day was health class. Before the bell rang, we found Mrs. Morse, our health teacher. We told her about our new plan and asked her for advice.

"Do you think that we should try to get the school to replace the soda machine with a juice machine?" I asked.

"Well, some juices have healthy vitamins, but even 100 percent fruit juice is high in calories," said Mrs. Morse. "And drinking too much juice can lead to weight problems. Juice machines usually sell fruit punch and sweetened ice tea too, which are full of sugar and other sweeteners and are just as bad as soda,"

Slim Goodbody Says: All 100 percent fruit juice and sports drinks are considered *Slow* drinks. The American Academy of Pediatrics, an organization that studies children's health, recommends that seven- to eighteen-year olds drink 12 ounces (1 1/2 cups or 355 ml) of juice or less a day. Lemonade, fruit punch, and juice drinks are considered *Whoa* drinks because they are high in sweeteners. Many of these drinks have less than 10 percent juice so they don't offer many nutrients either.

BETTER BEVERAGES

"What about water? It doesn't have any sugar or calories, but it keeps you **hydrated**," said Stacey.

"That's true," said Mrs. Morse.

"Low-fat and skim milk are good too, right?" asked Cameron.

"Absolutely. They are high in calcium, which is good for your skin, muscles, and bones. Whole milk, on the other hand, has quite a lot of **saturated fat**, which is bad for your heart," said Mrs. Morse.

"So what if we try to get the school to find a way to sell water and skim milk instead of soda?" I suggested.

"I think that sounds like a great idea!" said Mrs. Morse.

Just then, the bell rang, and we went to our desks.

Slim Goodbody Says: Compare these Nutrition Facts labels and decide which of these kinds of milk is a *Whoa* drink and which one is a *Go* drink.

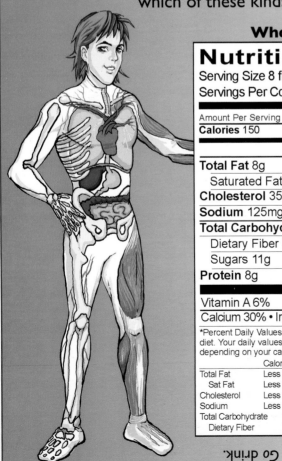

Whole Milk

Nutrition Facts

Serving Size 8 fl oz (240ml)
Servings Per Container 2

Amount Per Serving	
Calories 150	Calories from Fat 70

	% Daily Value*
Total Fat 8g	12%
Saturated Fat 5g	25%
Cholesterol 35mg	12%
Sodium 125mg	5%
Total Carbohydrate 12g	4%
Dietary Fiber 0g	0%
Sugars 11g	
Protein 8g	

Vitamin A 6%	•	Vitamin C 4%

Calcium 30% • Iron 0% • Vitamin D 25%

*Percent Daily Values are based on a 2,000 calorie diet. Your daily values may be higher or lower depending on your calorie needs.

	Calories	2,000	2,500
Total Fat	Less than	65g	80g
Sat Fat	Less than	20g	25g
Cholesterol	Less than	300mg	300mg
Sodium	Less than	2,400mg	2,400mg
Total Carbohydrate		300g	375g
Dietary Fiber		25g	30g

Skim Milk

Nutrition Facts

Serving Size 8 fl oz (240ml)
Servings Per Container 2

Amount Per Serving	
Calories 80	Calories from Fat 0

	% Daily Value*
Total Fat 0g	0%
Saturated Fat 0g	0%
Cholesterol less than 5mg	1%
Sodium 130mg	5%
Total Carbohydrate 12g	4%
Dietary Fiber 0g	0%
Sugars 11g	
Protein 8g	

Vitamin A 8%	•	Vitamin C 4%

Calcium 30% • Iron 0% • Vitamin D 25%

*Percent Daily Values are based on a 2,000 calorie diet. Your daily values may be higher or lower depending on your calorie needs.

	Calories	2,000	2,500
Total Fat	Less than	65g	80g
Sat Fat	Less than	20g	25g
Cholesterol	Less than	300mg	300mg
Sodium	Less than	2,400mg	2,400mg
Total Carbohydrate		300g	375g
Dietary Fiber		25g	30g

Answer: Whole milk is a *Whoa* drink, while skim milk is a *Go* drink.

TV AND SNACKING: A TERRIBLE TWOSOME

"That always happens to me. I sit down to watch my favorite shows with a bag of potato chips. Before I realize it, I've eaten the whole bag," admitted Dave, one of the boys in our class.

"All right, guys," said Mrs. Morse. "Today, we're going to talk about eating healthy snacks. How many of you like to eat snacks when you're watching TV?"

We all raised our hands.

"The problem with snacking in front of the TV is that you're distracted, so it's easy to eat too much. I mean, who looks for the serving size on their bag of the potato chips when they're watching TV? As a result, we eat more than we ought to," Mrs. Morse explained.

"In general, when kids watch TV, they snack on foods that are high in fat, cholesterol, salt, and sugar. Unfortunately, those snacks are also low in vitamins, minerals, and fiber," said Mrs. Morse.

"Sounds like *Whoa* snacks," whispered Cameron, with a grin.

"For sure," I nodded.

WHOA

SNACK SUGGESTIONS

"Eating too much food that is high in fat, cholesterol, salt, and sugar can lead to **obesity** and health problems like high cholesterol and heart disease. The best thing to do is to turn off the TV and be active outside. But since most of us won't give up watching TV altogether, how can we be sure to eat well in front of the television?" asked Mrs. Morse.

"Eat an apple instead of potato chips," suggested Dave.

"Or make a small bowl of a snack, and leave the rest of the package in the kitchen. If the bag isn't right in front of you, you won't eat as much," offered Jen, a girl in our class.

"You can also drink water while you watch TV. I never feel as hungry if I drink water," I said.

"Those are all great ideas," said Mrs. Morse. "You can also plan to watch TV just after you've eaten a meal. That way, you won't be hungry for a snack."

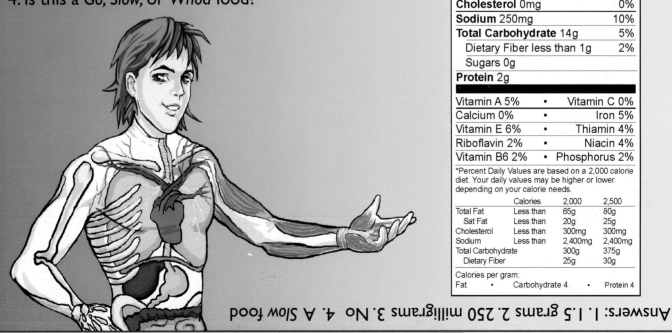

Slim Goodbody Says: Look at this Nutrition Facts label for spicy tortilla chips. Many young people eat this kind of snack while they're watching television. Can you answer the following questions?

1. How much saturated fat per serving does this snack contain?
2. How much sodium per serving?
3. Does it contain a significant amount of vitamins, minerals, and fiber?
4. Is this a *Go, Slow,* or *Whoa* food?

Nutrition Facts

Serving Size 1 oz (28g/About 21 pieces)
Servings Per Container about 2

Amount Per Serving	
Calories 170	Calories from Fat 110

	% Daily Value*
Total Fat 11g	17%
Saturated Fat 1.5g	8%
Trans Fat 0g	
Cholesterol 0mg	0%
Sodium 250mg	10%
Total Carbohydrate 14g	5%
Dietary Fiber less than 1g	2%
Sugars 0g	
Protein 2g	

Vitamin A 5%	•	Vitamin C 0%
Calcium 0%	•	Iron 5%
Vitamin E 6%	•	Thiamin 4%
Riboflavin 2%	•	Niacin 4%
Vitamin B6 2%	•	Phosphorus 2%

*Percent Daily Values are based on a 2,000 calorie diet. Your daily values may be higher or lower depending on your calorie needs.

	Calories	2,000	2,500
Total Fat	Less than	65g	80g
Sat Fat	Less than	20g	25g
Cholesterol	Less than	300mg	300mg
Sodium	Less than	2,400mg	2,400mg
Total Carbohydrate		300g	375g
Dietary Fiber		25g	30g

Calories per gram:
Fat • Carbohydrate 4 • Protein 4

Answers: 1. 1.5 grams 2. 250 milligrams 3. No 4. A *Slow* food

The Truth about Food Advertisements

"I don't know, Mrs. Morse. It doesn't matter if I just ate dinner, as soon as I see an **advertisement** for a hamburger or a candy bar, I want to eat it!" said Dave shaking his head.

"That's a great point," said Mrs. Morse, nodding. "Ads are made to convince you to buy a product. And about one-third of the ads on TV are for food. Advertisers have all sorts of tricks to make food look delicious so you'll want to go out and buy it."

 **Slim Goodbody Says:** Studies show that kids between the ages of eight and twelve watch about 21 food ads a day. That means that in one year, most kids will watch more than 7,000 food ads! That's over 50 hours of food advertisements each year!

"Yeah, and you never see ads for healthy snacks like a piece of fruit or carrot sticks. They're always trying to sell junk food!" said Stacey.

"That's right. Most food advertisements are for candy, sugary drinks, and unhealthy snacks like chips and ice cream," said Mrs. Morse.

16

Slim Goodbody Says: In a typical day, the average eight- to twelve-year old will see:

- 5 ads for candy and snacks
- 4 ads for high-fat foods
- 4 ads for soda and other soft drinks
- 3 ads for cereal
- 2 ads for restaurants
- 1 ad for prepared food, such as mini frozen pizzas or microwaveable macaroni and cheese
- 2 ads for the following categories combined: dairy, water, juice, meat, poultry, fish, fruit, vegetables, or grains

TRICKS OF THE TRADE

"Advertisers have all sorts of tricks, from painting food to arranging it perfectly, to make it look appealing. They also use slogans like 'low fat' or 'low cholesterol' to make you think that snacks are healthy even if they are high in calories and sugar. So don't let yourselves be fooled by advertisements. Use what you already know about eating **nutritious** snacks to make healthy choices about what you eat," Mrs. Morse told us.

After class, my friends went to Mrs. Morse's desk.

"Mrs. Morse, I just had another idea," I said. "What if we had a healthy snack sale to show kids how good healthy snacks can taste? We can sell snacks like fruit salad and celery sticks with peanut butter. Then maybe more students will agree that we should have healthier snacks in the vending machines."

"That's a great idea, Alexis. Let me know if I can help out," said Mrs. Morse.

Have a Healthy Snack!

The next week, our nutrition club met to plan our healthy snack sale.

"So what should we sell?" asked Stacey.

"I was thinking about bringing fruit-cicles," I said

"What are those?" asked Julia, a girl in our club.

"Have you ever tried frozen blueberries or frozen grapes? They are so good! All you have to do is put a toothpick in each piece of fruit and then freeze them for a couple of hours. Then you have your fruit-cicle!" I explained.

"I'm going to bring my famous salsa corn cheese sticks," said Cameron.

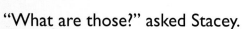

"What are those?" asked Stacey.

"They're awesome. All you have to do is wrap a stick of low-fat mozzarella cheese in a corn tortilla. Then you dip it in salsa and eat it!" said Cameron.

"That sounds really good," said Tim, one of the boys in our club. "I was thinking about bringing ants on a log."

"Those are celery sticks filled with peanut butter with raisins sprinkled on top, right?" I asked. "I love those."

DIPS AND POPS

Stacey said, "I think I'll make veggie dip. It's so easy. You just take 1 cup (250 ml) of non-fat yogurt and stir in ranch dressing mix or herbs like basil and garlic. Then you cut vegetables like broccoli, carrots, peppers, celery, and cauliflower into strips. Dip the strips for a tasty treat. What are you going to make, Julia?"

"I'm going to make pink-lemonade yogurt pops," Julia told us.

"Yum! How do you make those?" I asked.
"Easy! All you do is add 4 tablespoons (60 ml) of pink lemonade concentrate to 1 cup (250 ml) of plain non-fat yogurt. My mom has popsicle containers, but you can use paper cups too. You pour the yogurt mixture into the containers or cups and stick a popsicle stick in. You have to freeze them for a couple of hours, but they are totally tasty," Julia smiled.

"Awesome. I think we've got a plan," said Cameron.

Slim Goodbody Says: If you are looking for more recipes for healthy snacks, take a look at this website — www.bam.gov/sub_foodnutrition/index.html. It has all sorts of great ideas!

HOW CAN I MAKE HEALTHY CHOICES?

The next week, we set up our healthy snack sale next to the vending machines.

"We have to think like advertisers," I told my friends. "Let's arrange the food so it looks really good." We also hung posters that said 'Healthy snacks make you feel great!' and 'Low-fat snacks for your body and brain!'

Mrs. Morse came by and said, "Kids will be choosing between your snacks and the junk food in the vending machine. I thought my decision-making poster would be helpful too."

"Thanks!" we said.

MAKE HEALTHY DECISIONS
- Identify your choices
- Evaluate each choice and their consequences
- Identify the healthiest decision
- Take action
- Evaluate your decision

HEALTHY SNACK SALE!

DECIDING WHAT SNACK IS BEST

Just then, Dave from our health class walked up to the vending machine and started digging in his pockets for his change. He looked at the food in the vending machine and then looked over at our table of healthy snacks.

"Hmm, this is a hard choice," he said.

I laughed and pointed to Mrs. Morse's decision-making poster. "Just follow the steps to make your decision!"

"OK," he chuckled. "I guess my choices are these potato chips or your salsa corn cheese sticks. They both look like they'd taste good, but the potato chips have a ton of fat."

"The cheese sticks are low fat and full of healthy nutrients. Plus you'll have more energy if you eat them," said Cameron, grinning.

"I guess the cheese sticks are the healthy choice," Dave said, shrugging his shoulders.

"Now all you have to do is take action!" I told him. Dave gave us his change and picked up a few of the salsa, corn, cheese sticks.

"Wow, these really are good!" he said. "Too bad they aren't in the vending machine!" He looked back at the poster. "If I had to evaluate my choice, I'd say that eating the healthy snack was the way to go."

"Our first sale!" said Stacey, grinning. "If we keep this up, we really will convince the other students to want healthy snacks in the vending machines."

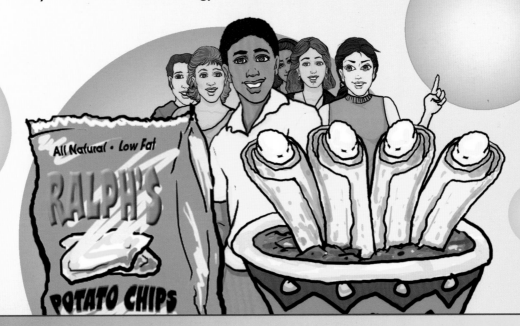

Slim Goodbody Says: Learning to make healthy choices is an important skill. Now it's your turn! Use Mrs. Morse's five steps for decision making to make healthy choices about the snacks you eat. Use the Nutrition Facts label and ingredients list on the back of the packages to compare your choices. Comparing labels makes it easier to find a *Go* snack!

GOOD GOALS GET GREAT RESULTS!

The next week, we were back in health class.

"I understand that you have to eat well to be healthy, but I love sweets. If there are cupcakes or cookies on the counter when I get home, I can't bring myself to eat an apple," Jen told the class.

Mrs. Morse nodded. "No one is perfect. We all have weaknesses. Why not try setting healthy goals so that you can work towards a healthier diet? Everyone please take out a blank piece of paper." As we did, she wrote down five steps on the board.

Goal Setting

1. Set a realistic goal and write it down

2. List the steps to reach the goal

3. Get help/support from others

4. Evaluate your progress

5. Reward yourself

Jen's Big Plan

Does anyone have an idea for a healthy goal they would like to set? Remember, it really helps if you set a goal for a specific amount of time, Mrs. Morse told us.

Jen raised her hand. I guess my goal is to eat healthy snacks when I get home from school for the next two weeks.

Great! Now what steps will you need to take to reach that goal, Jen? asked Mrs. Morse.

I can make a big fruit bowl and put it on the dining room table. That way, I won t even have to go into the kitchen for a snack, and I won t be tempted by the other treats on the counter, said Jen.

That sounds like a good plan. Will you need support from your friends and family? asked Mrs. Morse.

I can ask my parents to buy healthy snacks so I m not tempted by the junk food, said Jen.

And how will you evaluate your progress? asked Mrs. Morse.

If I eat a healthy snack, I ll put a fruit sticker on my calendar. After two weeks, I can see if I met my goal, Jen replied.

Great! And how will you reward yourself if you meet your goal? Remember, having healthy rewards is as important as setting healthy goals, said Mrs. Morse.

Hmm, I guess I ll treat myself to a movie with my friends for my reward, said Jen.

Great work, Jen, said Mrs. Morse.

Slim Goodbody Says: When you set healthy goals, it s easier to identify, adopt, and maintain healthy behavior. Use Mrs. Morse s five steps and set your own healthy goal. Maybe you can cut back on *Whoa* foods too!

23

Know When to Say No!

After we finished writing down our goals, Mrs. Morse said, "There will be times when you are tempted to make unhealthy choices. An important part of growing up is learning how to make healthy choices and sticking with them. You should never feel like making the healthy choice is wrong, no matter what the situation is. It can be helpful to use these four steps when you need to say 'no' to a friend."

As she spoke, Mrs. Morse wrote on the board.

"Let's say that you set a goal to eat healthier snacks, but your friends are still eating junk food after school. If they offer to share their candy bar or soda, how can you tell them that you would rather eat an apple?" asked Mrs. Morse.

"My friends would make fun of me if I told them I'd rather eat an apple than a candy bar," said Dave.

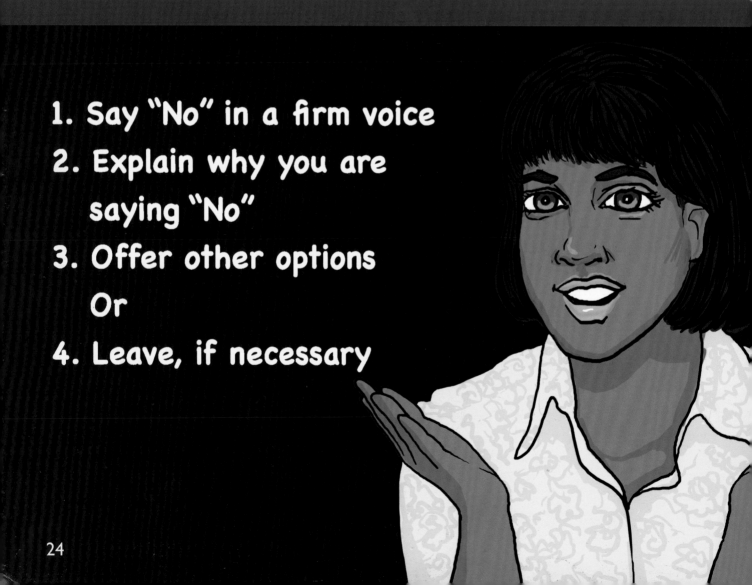

1. Say "No" in a firm voice
2. Explain why you are saying "No"
3. Offer other options
   Or
4. Leave, if necessary

The Pressure Is On

"It can be hard, but try using this tool. Imagine that you're in the store with your friends, and they ask if you want a candy bar."

Dave looked at the steps on the board. "I guess I would say, 'No thanks.'"

"And what if they ask why?" asked Mrs. Morse.

"I guess I'd tell them that I'd rather eat healthy food because I feel better when I do. I could also tell them that I am trying to get ready for basketball season. I need to eat food that builds my strength, not my stomach," said Dave with a chuckle, patting his belly.

"Great," said Mrs. Morse. "And would you offer other options?"

"Yeah. I keep a few apples or bananas in my backpack so that I have a healthy snack if I get hungry. I could offer to share one or two with my buddies. They would probably just laugh at me, though," said Dave.

"Well, if that's the case, you can simply walk away. Eventually, your friends will respect your decision. Who knows? They might even start eating better too. If they don't respect you after a while, they probably aren't very good friends," said Mrs. Morse. "Good work, Dave."

25

THE VENDING MACHINE VICTORY

The next week, our nutrition club had a meeting with our principal, Mr. Wilson, in our health classroom.

"Thanks for meeting with us, Mr. Wilson," I said. "We want to talk with you about the junk food in the vending machines. Did you know that 25 percent of the calories that kids eat come from snacks? That's why we think the school should sell nutritious snacks." I pointed to the *Whoa* Foods poster. "The cookies, candy and chips in the vending machines are *Whoa* foods. *Whoa* foods are high in fat and calories, but they don't have healthy nutrients."

Pointing to the *Slow* Foods poster, Stacey spoke up, "*Slow* foods, like crackers with low-fat peanut butter or raisins, have a medium amount of calories, fat, and sweeteners. They also have important vitamins, minerals, and protein. They'd be better to sell than the cookies and chips."

Cameron added, pointing to the *Go* Foods poster, "It would be best to offer *Go* foods that are low in calories, fat, sodium, and sugar and high in healthy nutrients. Packages of vegetable sticks, fruit cups, pretzels, and fat-free string cheese are all *Go* foods."

"We want to show kids that healthy snacks can taste great and give them more energy. Then they might eat healthier food when they watch TV at home or when they hang out with their friends," I told the principal.

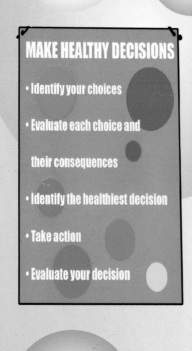

MR. WILSON RESPONDS

Mr. Wilson listened carefully to our presentation. "I think that you guys are on to something. I've been concerned about the food and drinks in the vending machines too. But do you think the other students will buy healthy snacks if we stock the vending machine with them?"

Stacey told him, "We had a healthy snack sale last week, and the students loved our food! Many of them said that they wished they could eat our snacks every day."

"I'm going to call the vending machine company this afternoon and ask for a list of their healthier snacks. Maybe you all can help me select snacks that are healthy and that the kids will enjoy," said Mr. Wilson.

"All right! Thanks, Mr. Wilson. Let us know when you need our help," I said happily.

 **Slim Goodbody Says:** What did you learn about healthy snacks from Alexis and her friends? Make a poster about what you discovered so that you will remember to choose *Go* foods for snacks in the future!

BE A HEALTH ADVOCATE!

A few weeks later, my brother Sam was back from college for the weekend. I found him in his room. "Hey, Sam. I wanted to tell you that our nutrition club had a healthy snack sale a couple weeks ago. Kids were lined up down the hall to buy our pink-lemonade yogurt pops and ants on a log!"

"Cool," said Sam.

"Not only that, but our principal, Mr. Wilson called the vending machine company. Now we only have healthy snacks in our vending machines!" I said happily. "We helped him choose nutritious snacks that the other kids would like."

A VOICE FOR HEALTHY CHANGE

"Alexis, you've really become a health **advocate**," said Sam.

"What's that?" I asked.

"A health advocate is someone who works to make their family, school, and community healthier and stronger. Health advocates *take a healthy stand on an issue*. Then they work *to persuade others to make a healthy choice*. And most importantly, they have to *be convincing*," explained Sam. "Does your nutrition club have any new projects?"

"Yes, our principal has already asked us to come with him to the next school board meeting. He wants to let other principals in the district know about what we did to get healthy snacks in our school."

"Do you think that you'll be able to persuade other schools to get healthy snacks in their vending machines too?" asked Sam.

"I think so. We're going to explain what we learned about the importance of healthy snacks and the health problems that kids experience when they eat unhealthy, pre-packaged snacks."

"Do you think you can be convincing?" asked Sam.

"You bet!" I said excitedly. "We're going to talk about our healthy snack sale and about how other students at our school like having the option to buy healthy snacks."

"That's really great, Alexis. It sounds like you really are working to make your community healthier and stronger," said Sam.

"Thanks, Sam. Hey, it's a beautiful day today. Do you want to go rock climbing?" I asked.

"I'd love to!" said Sam.

Slim Goodbody Says: Now it's your turn to become a health advocate. Help your family, friends, and community make healthier choices. Make your own poster about *Go, Slow,* and *Whoa* foods. Hang it in the hallway at school to teach other kids about eating healthy snacks. Does your school have vending machines too? Talk with your teacher about ways that your school can sell healthy snacks!

GLOSSARY

advertisement An announcement that gives information about and promotes a product or service

advocate A person who supports or speaks in favor of a cause or an idea

calcium A mineral found in milk and other foods that helps the body build strong bones and teeth

calories Units of energy contained in foods and drinks. Calories are used to produce energy. Extra calories not used as energy may be stored as fat.

cholesterol A fatty substance found in animal products. Meats, egg yolks, and dairy products, such as butter and cheese, contain cholesterol.

diabetes A disease in which a person has too much sugar in their blood. A person with diabetes cannot produce enough insulin, the substance the body needs to use sugar properly.

fiber Material in food that cannot be digested but helps with going to the bathroom

high blood pressure A condition that forces the heart to work harder to pump blood

hydrated Having enough water in the body

nutrients Chemical compounds (such as protein, fat, carbohydrate, vitamins, or minerals) that make up foods. The body uses nutrients to function and grow.

nutrition The study of food and diet

nutritious Describing foods that give the body energy and help it grow and heal

obesity A medical condition in which someone has a much higher amount of body fat than lean muscle mass

Percent Daily Value A section of the Nutrition Facts label that shows the amount of each nutrient in a serving of a food. It is usually based on a 2,000-calorie diet.

pre-packaged snacks Foods, such as macaroni and cheese, potato chips, and candy bars, that are prepared and packaged at a factory for quick and easy eating at home. To keep pre-packaged foods fresh, unhealthy preservatives and other chemicals are often added. In addition, pre-packaged foods are often high in fat, sugar, and calories.

saturated fat A fat that tends to be solid at room temperature. It is usually found in animal products such as beef, butter, and whole-fat milk and can cause heart problems and high blood pressure.

serving size A uniform amount of a food, such as a cup or an ounce, used to compare similar foods. Serving sizes are printed on the food label.

sodium Salt, which can cause high blood pressure

FOR MORE INFORMATION

Center for Disease Control: BAM! Body and Mind

www.bam.gov/sub_foodnutrition/index.html

Learn interesting facts and play games about nutrition and making healthy choices about the food that you eat.

Kidnetic

www.kidnetic.com

Learn new healthy and delicious recipes, play games, and find tips on staying fit and healthy on this website.

Kids Health for Kids: *Go, Slow,* and *Whoa*

www.kidshealth.org/kid/nutrition/food/go_slow_whoa.html

Learn more about the *Go, Slow,* and *Whoa* approach to eating and learn which foods are best.

Kids Health for Kids: When Snack Attacks Strike

www.kidshealth.org/kid/stay_healthy/food/snack_attack.html

Check out what to do when a snack attack strikes you.

United States Food and Drug Administration: Eat Smart Play Hard- Kids
www.fns.usda.gov/eatsmartplayhardkids

Play games, learn about making healthy choices, and discover how to prepare nutritious, delicious snacks.

INDEX

ABOUT THE AUTHOR

John Burstein (also known as Slim Goodbody) has been entertaining and educating children for over thirty years. His programs have been broadcast on CBS, PBS, Nickelodeon, USA, and Discovery. He has won numerous awards including the Parent's Choice Award and the President's Council's Fitness Leader Award. Currently, Mr. Burstein tours the country with his live multimedia show "Bodyology." For more information, please visit slimgoodbody.com